MW01257585

I THINK I NEED
A NEW HEART

The Journey From Heart Failure to Transplant

I THINK I NEED A NEW HEART

The Journey From Heart Failure to Transplant

by

Manu Kalia

MANUBRIUM BOOKS
A DIVISION OF VALINOR, INC.
NEW YORK   SAN FRANCISCO   WINTERFELL

Copyright © 2017 by Manu Kalia

All rights reserved. This book or any portion thereof may not be reproduced or used in any manner whatsoever without the express written permission of the publisher except for the use of brief quotations in a book review or scholarly journal.

First Printing: 2017

ISBN: 978-1-365-88161-9

Manubrium Books
17 Bagshot Row
Hobbiton, The Shire

For transplant professionals,
who wrestle the gift of life
from the tragedy of death untimely

For transplant patients, their caregivers,
friends, and families

And, of course,
for all organ donors and their loved ones

CONTENTS

I once heard a story about a terrifying, many-eyed demon who sat upon a boulder near a mountain trail in Tibet. He pounced on unsuspecting travelers, tearing them open from throat to groin, violently ripping out their desires and attachments with his claws. Then, he sent them on their way. I don't remember the demon's name, but the story has stayed with me.

On April 1st, 2016, my own chest was cut open, my heart scooped out, and replaced by that of a poor soul who could no longer use it. A tame bolt of lightning was applied to this stranger's heart, and then I too, was sent on my way.

This little book you're holding started out as a blog, intended to keep my family and friends updated as to the latest medical news on my condition. It was simply not going to be possible for my better half, Stephanie, and I to have individual text, email, and telephone correspondence with every single person who wanted to be kept updated.

Now that the dust has settled a bit, a full year and more after my first hospitalization, I've decided to write these words, and to include the actual blog entries as a chronology of my journey from catastrophic heart failure to heart transplant and recovery. During and after each of my two surgeries, Stephanie took over and wrote a few of the blog entries, so I've included those as she wrote them.

The blog entries are inserted here as originally written, with only minor editing to correct typos and bad grammar. The raw thoughts and emotions at the time were worth preserving and sharing, I thought. I also divided the blog entries into three distinct phases corresponding to my medical journey, and wrote some prose before and after each section of blog entries in order to wrangle the whole thing together into a somewhat coherent whole.

It's my hope that this short memoir is of interest and of value, primarily for heart failure patients who are facing the possibility or necessity for an LVAD (Left Ventricular Assist Device), and possibly heart transplantation. I know that I took tremendous comfort from the conversations I had with post-transplant patients back when I was first hospitalized. There's nothing quite like hearing the first-hand experiences, from someone who's been through the journey. I had attended, and still attend, a monthly VAD/transplant support group held at UCSF for transplant and VAD patients and their caregivers. I'm very grateful for this resource, and hope that this booklet can similarly provide a little bit of encouragement and reassurance.

In addition to patients and their caregivers, this memoir may also be interesting for the many professionals who work so dedicatedly in the transplant arena. A patient's perspective can be illuminating, even for deeply experienced experts. It's not always easy for the healthy to understand the sick. Like asking a shepherd-dog to understand a sheep. So I sheepishly offer this account.

Finally, it may be a mildly interesting story in general. Who knows? Certainly, it was a dramatic, albeit non-consensual, transformation for me. It's no exaggeration to say that my old life has ended, and new one has begun. It's also no exaggeration to say that I'm no longer under any illusion that I'm a separate entity. Not even all the organs in my body started with me.

Life, death, transformation, rebirth, interconnectedness. It's usually the area of prophets and philosophers, but sometimes the rest of us can weigh in. I leave it to others to judge, but here's my story.

A Sword of Damocles has hung over my head for my entire adult life. The ancient parable of the Sword of Damocles was popularized in the year 45 B.C.E. by Cicero, as a cautionary tale about the fragility of life and happiness.

According to legend, the ancient king and tyrant Dionysius II taught an unforgettable lesson to a fawning court flatterer, named Damocles. Dionysius taught Damocles what it would be like to be surrounded by luxury and riches, yet still be full of fear and misery. King Dionysius had Damocles bathed and pampered with rich foods, wine, and all manner of exotic luxuries. But Damocles couldn't help staring at the razor-sharp sword that King Dionysius caused to be hung above the head of Damocles—hanging by single, delicate strand of horsehair.

Fearing that his life might end at any moment, Damocles was not able to enjoy any of the fine luxuries before him. Life is indeed short for all of us. But for me, even more so. I always felt sure that I was doomed to a lingering death by age 45, the age at which my father died. That fear has always sat on my shoulder, leeching a little bit of joy from every moment in my life.

Paradoxically, one of the greatest joys of life after receiving an organ transplant is the gift of ignorance. I no longer feel I have any information about whether I will die tomorrow, or forty years from tomorrow. It makes getting up each day an act of exploration without dread.

My father died of congestive heart failure stemming from hypertrophic-cardiomyopathy, which most likely progressed to dilated-cardiomyopathy. Cardiomyopathies tend to be genetic, and during a routine college physical in 1991, doctors had found a heart murmur in me. Those were the words that started a nightmare journey for my father twenty years earlier, and dozens of little clues snapped into place in my mind. My barely-conscious, nagging little fears suddenly came into focus.

Although I had always been active and in pretty good shape, I always wondered why there seemed to be a ceiling on what I could accomplish, physically. Other athletes on my teams seemed to blossom with time and work, but not me. I peaked early. I feared to look too closely at what I knew to be the truth, and just told myself I needed to push harder.

Deep down, I knew I had my answer after that first echocardiogram at age 20. But I still clung to denial, even in the face of reality. Perhaps it was *benign* cardiomyopathy, I told myself. After all, many people have a heart wall thickening, but don't show any other symptoms, living their entire lives in ignorance of their condition. I developed a superstition: if I could just live to age 45 without heart failure (the age at which my father died), then I was in the clear. However, that was not to be. By the time I was about 42, the first signs of congestive heart failure had surfaced.

Congestive Heart Failure (CHF), is a spectrum of symptoms that describe what happens when the heart muscle begins to pump weakly or inefficiently. As a result, not enough blood, oxygen and nutrients circulate to the body and various organ systems, including the heart itself. To compensate, the heart's chambers may enlarge and distend, and the heart walls may thicken and become stiff. In response, the kidneys begin to retain water and salt in various parts of the body, such the lungs, the extremities, and elsewhere. Hence the term, *congestive*.

There are many ways to arrive at congestive heart failure: heart attack, coronary artery disease, chronic high blood pressure, infection, drug or alcohol abuse, congenital defects, valve defects, thyroid disease, and more. Over 6 million Americans are in some stage of CHF right now, with over 670,000 new diagnoses annually.

Many good online resources define CHF and provide information for the curious, so I'll just stick to symptoms and my own personal experience. For me, fatigue and weakness was dominant. It started very subtly, showing up as a feeling that I just didn't sleep well. My periodic jogs became harder.

Infrequently at first, and then chronically, I developed symptoms of acid reflux and loss of appetite. I lost 45 pounds in two years. Granted I was 30 pounds overweight to begin with, but still. Most painfully, as my lungs began to congest, I developed a dry, hacking cough that never went away. I could no longer lie flat to sleep. Fortunately, I was spared one of the other common symptoms of CHF, which is edema, or swelling of the extremities.

Echocardiograms over the years had shown a decline in my ejection fraction (a measure of the heart's pumping efficiency) from 50% at age 20, to 24% at age 42, and 18% at age 44. The normal, ideal ejection fraction range for a healthy heart is 60%-70%.

Under a cardiologist's care, I had been able to manage these symptoms with diuretics and a beta-blocker, but prudence suggested that I begin the process of getting cleared for heart transplant in the near future. I thought I was a couple years away from needing that drastic intervention, but why not get the process started, I thought. Why not let the team at UCSF (the center I selected because of its reputation and proximity) get to know me? It was a good thing my brother prodded me to get the transplant candidacy process started, because I didn't have nearly the time I thought I had.

Here is the first set of blog entries. My first hospitalization was on November 18th, 2015.

SO, WHAT'S THE DEAL?
27 NOV 2015

What's going on with you? How are you so sick and I don't know about it? Fair enough. The short answer is that I have a congenital heart condition called "left ventricular non-compaction cardiomyopathy with systolic disfunction," which is sometimes asymptomatic, but other times leads to congestive heart failure. Unfortunately, I have the second kind.

This is likely a condition that I've had since birth, and certainly for well over 20 years. It belongs in a class of heart conditions called cardio-myopathy.

To learn more, click on this link...
http://en.wikipedia.org/wiki/Noncompaction_cardiomyopathy

It's a condition my father had, and died from, in 1986 at age 45. He started to develop noticeable symptoms a few years earlier, at about age 41. I'm now 44, and I started to have noticeable shortness of breath a couple of years ago at 42. I haven't felt too bad for the last couple years, and have been controlling some of the symptoms with medication (carvedilol, a beta-blocker; and furosemide, a diuretic). But there is no question that I am on much the same disease pathway.

I've always had a weaker heart than most other people, but no particular symptoms other than not being able to achieve the physical athleticism I've always wanted. All in all, I can't really complain. I certainly had no pain, arrhythmia, or other symptoms for my first 42 years. Many people with cardio-myopathies aren't even aware they have them. Len Bias, the college basketball star who died suddenly in his twenties, is one example.

There is no cure for this condition. The proper long term destination is heart transplant. And that's the journey I'm on. There are a number of things that need to happen before transplant, but overall, my team of medical doctors at UCSF are very optimistic, and so am I.

THE ROAD TO HEART TRANSPLANT
28 NOV 2015

The only viable long-term treatment option, in my case, is heart transplant... the act of replacing one's heart with that of a recently-deceased donor's heart. Beyond being simply amazing that such a thing is possible, we happen to live in an age when heart transplantation is fairly well-practiced, and post-transplant life expectancy has become quite long in many cases.

There are a number of centers-of-excellence around the country and around the world. Luckily enough, UCSF (University of California, San Francisco) happens to be one of those places. Right in our back yard! I've met just about the entire team here, and have been deeply impressed by them. I've verified every step, every piece of logic, and every recommendation with people I trust, and I haven't been steered wrong in even the smallest thing.

A great many tests and hurdles need to be cleared before being listed as a transplant recipient waiting for a donor organ. Everything gets examined and evaluated by a large team: medical conditions of all kinds, psychological factors, social support network, financial circumstances, patient personality and attitude... you name it, they test it. If everything checks out, particularly on the medical front, then the candidate is cleared to be listed for transplant and begins waiting for a donor organ. The prioritization is mostly based on medical urgency.

WHAT HAS HAPPENED SO FAR
29 NOV 2015

As my second year on medication progressed, my condition slowly but steadily worsened. My brother, who has been an irreplaceable source of support and medical knowledge, advised me to start the long process of getting qualified for transplant, specifically at UCSF. Far better to do it in a reasoned and deliberate manner than needing to scramble if my condition became medically urgent.

Wiser words never were spoken. I've spent the last four months going through all of the different meetings, interviews, tests, and evaluations that are required to become a transplant candidate. Most everything has been smooth sailing. I'm relatively young (at least for heart transplant), am in otherwise excellent physical condition, have a fantastic support network of family and friends (this means you), and am 100% engaged in my own healthcare. It also turns out that as blood type AB, I can receive a donor heart from any blood type donor. As an average sized individual, I also don't have particular restrictions on the size of the donor organ.

It all sounded so promising.

but…

In what I thought would be a routine procedure (called right heart catheterization), my doctors discovered a pronounced case of pulmonary hypertension. This right heart cath procedure is the only real way to measure the pressures in the blood vessels around the heart and lungs. It involves threading a thin wire directly into the area of the heart, via the jugular vein in the neck.

My doctors admitted me into the hospital, where I stayed for the next six nights. I was discharged the day before Thanksgiving, with a home IV infusion kit, and a defibrillation vest.

Pulmonary hypertension is a high blood pressure in the vessels between the heart and lungs. In my case, prolonged weakness in the left ventricle's pumping action has led to a type of compensatory pumping from the right ventricle. This is apparently the wrong direction, and in response, the blood vessels in my lungs have contracted to resist this unnatural flow of blood. Bottom line, I cannot have a transplant until this pulmonary hypertension is resolved. Putting a donor heart into my body right now would lead to failure of the new organ because of my pulmonary hypertension.

There is a drug-based treatment for pulmonary hypertension (the drug is called Milrinone) that my team has tried over the past week, and on which I continue at home by IV. The drug alone, over a short period of time, was not likely to lower pulmonary hypertension significantly. And indeed it didn't, as shown by a second right heart cath procedure.

For my circumstance, the much surer method of resolving pulmonary hypertension would be to implant a mechanical pump into my chest, replacing the weakened left ventricle's pumping action. This device is called a left ventricular assist device (LVAD), and that's what I'm about to have implanted. It's a bit bigger than a golf ball, and has a wire that will poke out of my abdomen to be connected to a controller and batteries. Tony Stark would be jealous.

I go bionic as soon as possible, hopefully by the second week of December 2015. It will take a month to recover from the surgery, and another couple of months for the pulmonary hypertension to resolve. By end of March 2016, I hope to be not only feeling better than I have in a couple of years, but also expect to be listed as a high-priority transplant candidate.

THE PLAN AS OF NOVEMBER 30TH
30 NOV 2015

The one obstacle that stands in the way of my immediate listing on the transplant wait list is my pulmonary hypertension. As mentioned, the next step is to have the major surgical procedure of LVAD implantation. The recovery from this implantation is two weeks in the hospital, followed by two weeks at home.

It is a long and painful recovery, but the results will be worth it. I'll need a lot of help, as will Stephanie, and we're both so grateful that everyone we've talked to has gone overboard with sincere offers to help out in any way we need.

I'm hoping to schedule my LVAD implantation during the second week of December, so I can be home before Xmas, and be back to work and feeling good by the second week of January 2016.

For the first 3-4 days after the implantation surgery, I will be in the cardiac ICU. It won't be easy to visit me there, and I'll likely be quite out of it and in great pain. By the second week, back in a normal hospital room, I may be up for visits for those of you nearby. Once I'm back home, I expect that I will start to improve steadily. Stephanie will probably need some help during the period from around Christmas through the first week of January. Stay tuned for more detail on what this might be!

The LVAD's augmentation/replacement of my left ventricular pumping action should start to ameliorate my pulmonary hypertension right away, but it will be about three months before the blood vessels in the lungs will relax and recover from the stresses that they have been put through. In mid- or late-March, I will have a third right heart cath procedure. When the elimination of my pulmonary hypertension is confirmed, I will be listed for heart transplant as a candidate in a high-medical-priority category (status 1-B).

One can't, of course, predict what the availability of donor hearts will be, so the wait could be anywhere from a few days to several months. In my case, there would be no particular urgency from a health perspective. Present day LVADs have become truly amazing in their longevity and effectiveness. I, of course, hope for a short wait for a donor heart.

When a donor organ does become available, I will undergo a second major surgery: the transplant. This a 6-12 hour procedure that is complex, but something that has come to be a nearly 100% successful operation. I've met the transplant surgeon who does all of the LVAD implantations and heart transplants at UCSF. He's done hundreds of each, and I feel I'll be in very good hands.

The recovery from transplantation is two weeks in the hospital, followed by four weeks of recuperation at home. Also a very hard recovery. And for six months afterword, there will be very frequent trips back to UCSF to manage immune suppressing drugs, rejection, and possible infections. I'll need lots of help and support during both recoveries, and feel so lucky and grateful to have the people in my life that I do. People who have already showered me with their kind wishes and offers of help and support. I can't say thank you enough, or often enough. Thank you thank you thank you.

By about a year after transplant, I expect to feel better than I have for years, and look forward to a nice long life thereafter. I aim to be a support and comfort to everyone else in my life, just as they have so generously given of themselves to me.

The very idea of an implanted pump is very off-putting. Rather like becoming a Borg on Star Trek. Worse, even, than the idea of a piece of hardware inside your body, is the fact that there will be a tube protruding from your abdomen, connected to three bricks that you carry around everywhere... two batteries and a control unit. And if both batteries die, so do you.

Oh, to be forced to let go of the illusion of independence. Sure, we all admit intellectually that we are all dependent on many things in our daily lives... electricity, food, housing, roads and bridges, sewage and sanitation systems. Like most of us, I clung in vain to the false idea that I was a strong, free, and fully independent being. Able to go anywhere, to do anything. It may be a falsehood, but even this comfortable illusion shatters when you have a wire sticking out of you, and you need to change batteries every 8 hours.

No, I most certainly did NOT want an LVAD. And yet, it most definitely saved my life. My heart was failing, and without a transplant, I would most certainly die. As a side-effect of my body's compensation for my heart's weakened pumping action, I had developed severe pulmonary hypertension. That eliminated me as a good candidate for cardiac transplant. A catch-22 if there ever was one.

Enter the amazing LVAD. By assisting my heart with blood circulation (relieving the left ventricle of its systolic load), an LVAD improves blood profusion to the brain, kidneys, liver, and rest of the body. Most importantly for me, my LVAD allowed my pulmonary artery to relax enough to permit cardiac transplantation.

The implantation of left-ventricular assist device allows not only it's immediate alleviation of CHF symptoms, but also removes the life-or-death urgency from the uncertain wait for an available donor organ. The LVAD carries the load of the failing heart, vastly prolonging the life of the heart failure patient.

LVADs were in their infancy in 1986 when my father lay in end-stage congestive heart failure. The absence of widely available and reliable LVAD technology made saving his life impossible. Timing is everything. LVAD technology has come a very long way during the 40 years from its invention in 1966 to 2016. What was an impossible catch-22 for my father, was eminently treatable for me.

Up through the 1990s, LVADs were the size of a small car, and prolonged a bed-ridden patient's life only by a matter of days or weeks. In the next 25 years, the size of the exterior drive unit shrunk to the that of a roll-aboard suitcase, then to that of a backpack, and today to the size of a brick. The implanted pump size has decreased to the point where it can be entirely implanted in the apex of the heart itself, no longer needing a pocket in the abdomen. Reliability has gone from ten days to seven years, and sometimes longer.

And the future brings even more dazzling improvement. There are versions of devices currently in clinic trials that are *half* the size of my Heartware HVAD device, and whose exterior batteries and controller are also half the size of what I needed to lug around. Even more exciting is the work on transdermal charging, in which the interior pump is charged through the skin, eliminating the need for a driveline exiting the abdomen, with its attendant risks of infection.

The advancements in the technology have moved LVADs into the typical status of the Bridge to Transplant. In cases of older patients, for whom transplant is not an option, LVADs have become a destination therapy, allowing for an active, good quality of life at home, for years. And surprisingly, LVADs have also been shown in some cases, to allow a damaged heart to recover enough to allow the LVAD to be removed (explanted). A bridge to recovery!

The small size of the modern LVAD allowed my surgeon to employ a less invasive implantation procedure. Rather than a full sternotomy, or cutting of the sternum, he used an incision in the left side of the rib cage, a mini-thoracotomy, to insert the device itself, and a mini-sternotomy, a 3 inch incision in the sternum, to access the aorta, to which the output tube from the LVAD was grafted. This minimal invasiveness allowed for a 15-day hospital stay, rather than the months it used to require.

Sounds easy, right? It wasn't, of course. There were unexpected twists in my post-surgical recovery, and for some people I've talked to in my support group, the recovery after LVAD implantation has taken months. Recovery from such a major surgery, which includes time on a heart-lung bypass machine, would be difficult for a perfectly healthy person. But for someone whose body has been weakened by months or years of congestive heart failure, it should come as no surprise that recovery is tough.

For me, it was a constant process of letting go. Letting go of the illusion of strength and independence. Letting go of control. Letting go of modesty, even. When you need help with, or need to plan a tactical campaign around using the toilet, there is no clinging to old notions of propriety! Luckily, all of these things are illusions and self-deception, so letting go of them wasn't really painful once forced to do so.

At one point in my hospital stay, a clot or drug interaction caused neurological symptoms: paranoia, inability to distinguish waking reality from a dream state, and motor-control and cognitive impairment. For a time, I was even forced to let go of sanity and intelligence, things I had always thought were the foundation of my identity.

Two things have come to me from that time of terror. First, I have great sorrow and sympathy for those who suffer from dissociative mental illness. To be trapped in one's own mind is a terrible thing. Second, I no longer know who I am. I have lots of memories, skills, and aptitudes that are useful. But what is an identity really?

Aside from the post-surgical journey to mobility and health, there is also the practical adjustment to life with an LVAD. It requires a re-engineering of one's home and one's life. We had to rearrange furniture, making sure the wall plug-in for my LVAD controller was adjacent to the bed. The battery charger needed to be arranged just so, also next to the bed. Our poor dog was kicked out of the bed, because there was no longer room for her, what with batteries and a controller that had to lie to my right. No showering, only sponge baths for three months. Remembering to always, ALWAYS carry the heavy backpack of spare batteries and controller whenever leaving the house.

Every morning, I had a new 90 minute routine, starting with a whole battery of tests... from weight, to blood-pressure, to temperature, to LVAD controller readings. Then, transmission of all those stats to a monitoring service in Florida. After that, taking a cocktail of drugs, including a high dose of blood thinners to prevent clots (a major risk factor with an LVAD). Pin pricks every two days to measure INR (clotting speed). Weekly visits to the clinic.

Post-LVAD life also requires good care at home, and good social support from family and friends. Stephanie changed my driveline dressing every third day, requiring her to get good at maintaining a sterile field. The driveline emerging from my abdomen was connected directly to my heart. Any infection at that driveline site would be life-threatening.

It was indeed a difficult recovery, and a difficult adjustment. But it was also the necessary next step on the road to transplant. And once I did recover from the surgery (about four weeks in total), I felt better than I had in years! I feel immense gratitude for the LVAD. I no longer had fluid in and around my lungs, I could sleep lying flat, and I could walk for miles. Most importantly, within three months, I was able to be listed as a candidate for cardiac transplant. Despite the physical weight of the LVAD controller, the batteries, and the spares, I felt light and free.

Here now are the blog entries relating to the LVAD implantation and recovery.

CHOICES ... CHOICES
04 DEC 2015

Well, things are never 100% clear, are they? And some choices are both high-stakes *and* low-information. I've been told that there has not been

clear consensus among my team of physicians at UCSF about the immediate short-term decision: whether to implant the LVAD right away, or to wait a month to give the medication (Milrinone) time to perhaps lower my pulmonary hypertension without an implanted device. In both cases, our goal would be to get me listed as a transplant candidate as soon as possible, since that is the best (and only) long term solution for me.

All-in-all, it would be really great to avoid the major surgery and recovery that is the reality of LVAD implantation.

On the other hand, the drug Milrinone is known to increase the risk of arrhythmia and ventricular tachycardia (requiring defibrillation), while at the same time, holding perhaps a 20% chance of reducing the pulmonary hypertension. If it didn't work, I'd need to get an LVAD anyway, and I've now added risk and about a month to my total treatment time.

It falls on me to make this choice, knowing that excellent physicians are honestly disagreeing about the best course of action. Thanks again to my brother Amit and his network of mentors and advisors. I feel that I have been given all the relevant information, as well as sage advice.

I'm tempted to give the Milrinone another month, as a chance to avoid the major LVAD implantation procedure. Also, I'd be able to go to the opening night of The Force Awakens. But, I think the risk of arrhythmia for a less-than-50% chance of success has pushed me to choose to undergo the LVAD surgery immediately (December 10th).

LVAD SURGERY POSTPONED
06 DEC 2015

It's not easy to change one's mind about a major decision. Once I made my choice last Thursday to proceed with the LVAD implantation, I felt a great relief to have this difficult decision behind me. But then of course, I kept thinking, and listening to expert opinions, and hearing good advice.

Naturally, I did a pros-and-cons list. As of Sunday, Dec. 6th, 2015, I've decided to postpone the LVAD implantation. I want to give the Milrinone a bit more time to work, before moving ahead with the LVAD surgery.

At a minimum, I'd like to consult with the head of the Transplant Center at UCSF, which I will only be able to do on Dec. 10th. That will mean at least one week's postponement, which will bring me to a total of three weeks on the drug Milrinone. Once I've given it this much time, it doesn't make much sense to NOT take another couple of weeks on the low-but-real chance (about 20%) that I might avoid the LVAD implantation step altogether. In that happy scenario, I would move directly to the transplant candidate list. It will all come down to whether the Milrinone is successful in reducing my pulmonary hypertension to acceptable levels.

There is a downside to waiting on the LVAD surgery, which is the slightly elevated risk of an arrhythmia. By using a 24x7 defibrillation vest, I think that this added risk is acceptable in the face of the tremendous benefit to avoiding a major open-heart surgery. The other benefit of avoiding the LVAD surgery is that having an "untouched" heart cavity with no scarring will make the eventual transplant surgery that much easier for the surgeons.

Stay tuned for the latest developments!

ONE MORE DATA POINT
10 DEC 2015

My brother, Amit, was able to fly out here to San Francisco this week to join me and Stephanie at my meeting with Dr. Teresa Demarco, the head of the UCSF Heart & Lung Transplant Center. It was great to have them both there. Amit's medical expertise as an interventional radiologist has been invaluable throughout my health travails.

At UCSF, Dr. Demarco was terrific, and spent a great deal of time with me, explaining what was going on in my heart and lungs, helping me make sense of the measurements, and walking me through all the risks and trade-offs of waiting vs. immediate LVAD implantation.

My biggest take-away was a better sense of the risks of an additional heart surgery on the later transplant surgery, contrasted against the risks of proceeding to transplant with anything less than excellent pulmonary pressures. It's become clear to me that the pulmonary hypertension absolutely *must* be controlled.

As for waiting a week before deciding, the meeting reinforced what we had been thinking, and confirmed our current plan. We will wait one more week before deciding whether an LVAD is needed. The critical new data point will come from another right heart catheterization.

This catheterization procedure will be my third measurement of internal pulmonary pressures and cardiac output. It will have been 4 full weeks after the start of Milrinone therapy, and should provide good data about whether the medication alone is making enough progress reducing the pulmonary hypertension to acceptable levels. If not, the LVAD implementation will be necessary as a bridge to transplant.

The right heart cath is scheduled for Wednesday, Dec. 16th, 2015. The best result (albeit the least likely), is to learn that the pressures are dropping at good rate, and we can move to listing me directly for transplant. The more likely scenario would be to observe *some* drop in pulmonary pressures, but not enough to make transplant a success. High pulmonary pressures will cause a new, healthy heart to fail almost immediately.

If pressures remain high, we will move to scheduling an LVAD implantation surgery. It could happen as early as Thursday, Dec. 17th. Yikes! If I wanted to clear the holidays and make sure the full "A-team" was back at their posts, I might push the surgery out 3 weeks to something like January 7th. With an implanted LVAD heart pump, I would be ready for listing as a transplant candidate in mid-April, most likely.

We'll certainly know a lot more on Wednesday, Dec. 16th.

FOR THE CURIOUS...
14 DEC 2015

In case anyone is wondering about the actual gear that I might have implanted in my chest, it is the Heartware HVAD device. To learn more, click over to their website, where there are lots of good descriptions and videos... http://heartware.com

I'd still love to skip the LVAD implantation step entirely and go right to transplant, but that isn't the likely scenario. So, I've begun to familiarize myself with the Heartware device, trying to get used to the idea.

RED FIVE, STANDING BY...
16 DEC 2015

I went in for my third right-heart-catheterization today. I'm starting to feel like a pro at this. I was a little disappointed to learn that my pulmonary pressures had not dropped enough from drugs alone to go directly to transplantation. Instead, as has always been more likely, I will need to undergo an LVAD implantation. Three months after that, we will do yet another right-heart-cath to confirm that my pulmonary pressures have moderated enough to be listed as a cardiac transplant candidate.

It's now down to a question of *when* to schedule the surgery. I was thinking that the first week of January would be ideal. My doctors, however, don't see any reason to wait, and told me that holiday schedules for the staff won't really make a difference. They basically work all the time, and on all the holidays. So, they are suggesting Tuesday, Dec. 22nd as the surgery date, with my pre-admittance being on Monday, Dec. 21st.

I'm a bit scared about the recovery process, but that is unavoidable. And putting it off won't make anything about the recovery the slightest bit easier.

Since I've met my primary objective of seeing the new Star Wars movie on Friday (9:30 am, baby!), I suppose I will listen to my medical team and go in for the surgery next Tuesday. I'm updating the EVENTS portion of this website accordingly.

Wish me luck, but more importantly, <u>MAY THE FORCE BE WITH MY SURGICAL TEAM!!</u> Let's hope they're well-rested and feeling bright-eyed & bushy-tailed on Tuesday!

KIDNEY BEANS
18 DEC 2015

Small modification to the plan. Instead of going in on Monday for pre-op admission, I went in this afternoon. One of my kidney function numbers, creatinine, is a bit high. Most likely, this is due to poor blood flow to the kidneys by the weak heart.

My docs want to keep the Tuesday surgery time slot, so they're taking the weekend to bring down my creatinine by upping my Milrinone dosage in a controlled setting. No big deal. Just means sitting around in the hospital an extra couple of days.

Unfortunately, I'll be missing a couple of fun social events this weekend. I plan to make up for it in the near future, though! The critical update is that I still got to see The Force Awakens this morning! Whew! It … Was… Awesome !!

LVAD SURGERY BEGINS
22 DEC 2015 (ENTRY BY STEPHANIE)

After a mini traffic jam at the UCSF elevators, Manu went into pre-op around 8:15am PT this morning. They wheeled him into the operating room around 9am.

Since the surgery is slated to take at least six hours, I won't hear from the doctor until 4pm or 5pm today. Anticipate another blog post around 5pm-7pm tonight.

In pre-op, we met several of the cardiac anesthesiologists and nurses who each asked about loose teeth, allergies and the purpose of his OR visit. We learned that at any given time there will be five people minimum in with the surgeon and at the most, eight. That's quite a team!

They repeatedly assured us that Manu would do great in surgery and that the LVAD would make him feel like a new person. One of the nurses told us the story of a woman with an LVAD who, agreeing to her doctor's orders not to ride horses, decided to ride a camel instead. So, Manu may soon take up camel racing with his bionic heart.

Thanks to everyone for all your visits, phone calls, texts, good vibes and declarations of The Force.

LVAD SURGERY DONE! MANU IS DOING GREAT!
22 DEC 2015 (ENTRY BY STEPHANIE)

Manu tolerated the LVAD surgery very well and there were no complications. He was taken down to Cardiac ICU around 3:30pm and I saw him around 5pm. He's still heavily drugged and intubated with a breathing tube going down his throat. I spoke briefly with one of his cardiologists who then spoke via phone with Amit, Manu's brother, who is also a doctor. They spoke the language of Doctor together and the scoop is that Manu's vitals are already improving due to the device.

Tomorrow, Amit and I plan to speak with the surgeon in the morning and then I'll see Manu shortly thereafter. I'm hoping that he'll be less sedated and have the tracheal tube out so he can speak a bit.

Everyone get out the bubbly since one of the biggest hurdles to getting a heart transplant is done. I'm celebrating with a gin and tonic in a 1983 Return-of-the-Jedi-Princess-Leia-Gold-Bikini commemorative glass, a gift to Manu by Wylie, one of Manu's partners in crime.

OF TUBES AND TINSEL
26 DEC 2015 (ENTRY BY STEPHANIE)

Manu is out of the ICU as of late Christmas evening and in a regular room on the cardiac floor at UCSF. Since the surgery on the 22nd, he's been getting stronger and more alert with each day.

He did very well in the ICU. Both doctors and nurses repeatedly remarked how fabulous he was doing post-op. Manu didn't feel fabulous (nor was he ready for his Hollywood close-up), but modern painkillers appeased his pain and discomfort. He was very groggy in the ICU and I think he won't have many memories of his stay there. He more than likely won't even remember Kona, the therapy dog, visiting his room.

I still haven't directly spoken with the surgeon, but have heard from the cardiologist that the surgery went very smoothly and quickly.

In the ICU post-LVAD surgery, it's all about taking out a tube or line each day. They achieved this with Manu, but in the beginning there were a total of at least 20 IV lines, cords, tubes, and sensors on or in Manu's body.

Manu will stay about another 10 days in the hospital, learning how to live with the LVAD, submitting to endless tests and blood draws, walking up and down the hallway with his Festivas IV pole, and eating low-salt hospital food. Then it will be home for another two weeks of more rest and rehab. After that, get ready for LVAD-propelled camel races to the nearest oyster bar.

ALMOST ... THERE ... STAY ... ON ... TARGET
29 DEC 2015

It has certainly been quite a week! All my docs tell me I've been recovering very well, and my surgical team was over-the-moon with how well the mini-thoracotomy technique worked. That was their expectation, but it's nice when a plan comes together. Just a quick note to thank you all for your good wishes. I expect to feel better and better from here on. There might be the occasional set-back, but it should be upwards from here.

STILL IN HOSPITAL
04 JAN 2016 (ENTRY BY STEPHANIE)

Yes, we're still in the hospital. Eighteen days and counting. We were hoping to get Manu home by the first of the year, which would have been a nice start to 2016. However, Manu's coumadin levels were not within the desired zone (coumadin is a blood thinner/anti-coagulant that prevents blood clotting which is a major concern with LVADs). In addition to that, Manu has not been feeling 100% so the doctors have been cautious and are performing some tests. This has added extra delays prior to discharge. We certainly hope to get home as soon as possible.

THERE'S NO PLACE LIKE HOME!
07 JAN 2016

I've clicked my ruby slippers, and at long last, on the afternoon of Wednesday, Jan. 6th, 2016, it happened. Like Gen. Douglas MacArthur to Corregidor, I have returned (home). It was a post-surgical hospital stay of 15 days, and a total of 18 days of hospitalization.

Just after the operation itself things were looking almost too good to be true. I had sailed through the operation, and the surgeons were pleased as cats eating canaries. My recovery was also rapid, and multi-organ response was very positive.

However, things took a hard left-turn into the darkness a few days after transferring from the ICU to the normal cardiac care floor. Around December 27th or so. I had had some trouble already with the awakening of my gut from the anesthesia (typically the last system to come out from under anesthesia).

As a result, I had developed an *illeus*, which is a twisting of the intestine. Vomiting in my then condition was considered quite dangerous, and several new anti-emitics were administered. I was on quite a cocktail of pharmacological agents by this time.

I began to experience neurological symptoms: hand-twitching, limb-spasms, confusion, inability to distinguish a sleep-state from waking reality; left-side right-side motor imbalance. I don't remember much of this period, but Stephanie saw it all. Teams of neurologists and surgeons frothing

25

around my bed, demanding a grin, a scowl, follow my finger, squeeze my hand, "what day is it?", "do you know where you are?"

I also remember feeling paranoid and suspicious. A head CT scan was completely clear, and there was no evidence of seizures or blood clots. So theories abound, but we'll never know what really happened. Let's just call it "drug-induced dementia."

I did emerge from that state, and since then, my recovery has been rapid. I got out of the hospital as soon as they would let me. I'm eating well, have strong appetite, and now starting to walk around. I've turned a corner and want everyone to know how much I appreciate their good wishes and prayers. Also, this is why we didn't encourage much hospital visitation. Now that I'm home and getting stronger, I'd love to see people as they have time to come by for visits. Life at home is so much better than the hospital, I've been in a mild state of euphoria for the last 24 hours. And that's not any drugs talking!

GETTING BACK TO NORMAL
20 JAN 2016

It's been 14 days since I shakily emerged from the hospital. 30 days since my LVAD implantation surgery. I'm very happy to share that my recovery has been profound and rapid over the last two weeks. My incisions are healing nicely, and I have a detailed regimen of measurements to perform every morning: weight, temperature, blood pressure, pulse, blood clotting speed, and LVAD operating metrics (pump revolution speed, pumped blood flow rate, and pump power consumption). I also have quite the cocktail of pills to take every morning and evening.

I'm also asked to listen to my heart (avec pump) every morning with a stethoscope. Instead of the lump-LUMP we're all familiar with, I hear a pulsating machine whine. It might be upsetting to some, but I find it totally bizarre and cool! Ain't technology grand? I also don't have an easily-measurable pulse, since the LVAD pushes blood though my body continuously, and not with periodic contractions. Pretty freaky. I cannot feel a pulse in my neck or wrists! I can only feel a pulse if I stick a finger into the hollow behind my collar-bone.

My numbers look good, and my medical team is pleased. They are not requiring me to come in as often now that I'm getting self-sufficient. In fact, Stephanie no longer needs to supervise me 24×7, or get a back-up baby-sitter if she wants to go to yoga, or get coffee with a friend. My undying gratitude to Stephanie, who has put in a yeoman's effort these past weeks. I'm not sure I'll be able to make it up to her… except perhaps with a LOT of Mitchell's Ice Cream!

I still am not allowed to drive, since an airbag deployment into my partially-healed mini-sternotomy wound would be fatal. I've got two more weeks of healing, and then the SmartCar goes a-cruising!

I suppose that it's more dramatic to write about hurdles to overcome, and suffering to endure. But I'm quite pleased to bore everyone with tales of joy and plenty and peasants dancing in the streets.

It is true that when I first got home from the hospital, I looked like a WWII prisoner-of-war released from the swamps of Malaysia. But I've put on some weight, regained some of my atrophied muscle mass, and have been eating and drinking up a storm (non-alcoholic drinks only, for now). I also have tried to walk longer and longer distances each day, or every other day.

I'm now up to ½ to ¾ miles over level ground before I get winded. And I can make it up all 25 stairs from the street in front of our house to our doorstep. I do need to catch my breath at that point, but that was a nice milestone to achieve.

I'm looking forward to more and more activity and a resumption of my disrupted life. I've been working this past week, and am feeling strong enough to put in almost a full day. Paco still needs his siesta, though! I had a lot of fun during one of our brief breaks in the rain recently. We took our doggy Stella to our local park, Glen Canyon.

I've got to carry some obnoxiously bulky batteries and a brick-of-a-controller around on a utility belt, but I shouldn't complain. I'm lucky not only to be alive, but also to be comfortable, at home, and living a pretty normal life!

Thanks to everyone that has paid us visits over the past few weeks. I look forward to more socializing over the next weeks and couple of months. I'm living in the moment for right now, refusing to think about what happens in April or thereabouts, with the big Step Two... the transplant. For now, I'm content to frolic in the park and play with sticks that are far too big for my body...

SIX WEEKS AFTER LVAD SURGERY ... LIVING THE GOOD LIFE
04 FEB 2016

I thought I'd write a quickie update, since it's been a while since the last posting, and people are curious about how things are going. I'm happy to say that everything is going as well as we could hope or imagine. My incisions are healing well and without infection. Appetite and

energy are good. Stamina back to pre-LVAD levels (not great by normal person standards, but good for someone in heart failure).

I've been putting in nearly a full workday, every day. Days in which I walk roundtrip to and from BART generally get me 2+ miles on my step-counter. And now, I'm cleared to drive! So the SmartCar is once again going to cruise the streets of San Francisco.

Mom was here last week for a marathon 8 days of cooking Indian food all day every day. Yumm! She thought she had packed our fridge with pre-made food and leftovers to last a couple of weeks. Hah! It's been six days, and the food is basically gone.

At any rate, I am now half-way through my three months of time needed to give my body a chance to relax from a couple years of heart failure. During the last week of March, I'll be going in for the right-heart  cath to verify that my pulmonary hypertension has resolved. Then, I await the phone call informing me that a donor organ is available. After that, about 6 weeks of difficult recovery again. Not thinking about that too much.

In the meantime, many people are visiting and coming over for fun meals. In a few weeks, Stephanie and I will join some friends in Tomales Bay for a long weekend of gourmet food and general debauchery. Various of my peeps are visiting from the East Coast in Feb and March. Fun, fun, fun!

Anyone in the area who wants to join us in some old-fashioned hedonism, give us a yell! Particularly if it involves sushi or raw oysters. Both of those foods will be off limits to me post-transplant, for the rest of my life (I'll be immune-suppressed, so no risks with bacteria).

If you swing by the house, you can use my stethoscope to listen to the bionic heart. It's totally cool... no heartbeat! Just a mechanical, pulsating hum. Matt, our local music maestro, has identified the machine hum as a natural E-note. Thank you everyone for your continued good wishes. We hope to see you soon!

After a few months with the LVAD, as my thoughts turned to the transplant procedure, my friend Terrie asked me if I had any help in coping with the uncertainty of waiting for a donor organ to become available. Did I have a therapist? I assured her that I would indeed seek out a professional if I felt the need, but that I really didn't feel anxiety about the wait.

I'm not sure if she believed me, but her concern warmed me. The truth is, waiting for transplant can be a very conflicted and ambiguous time for a transplant candidate. Every individual is different, and every situation is different, of course. Someone waiting for a kidney donor, having been on painful and debilitating dialysis for years will probably feel very anxious. Anyone waiting for a lung or liver donor, looking at the possibility of death at any time, most likely feels near to panic. For a heart transplant candidate with an LVAD supporting heart function, the situation is more clouded.

I could never feel comfortable with the knowledge that a successful transplant for me could only occur with the death of someone else. That is an inescapable truth. I certainly hated the idea that I would so benefit from another person's death. But there was no denying that I very much wanted to live.

One of the many, many tests and consultations on the way to being approved as an organ transplant candidate at UCSF is sitting with a social worker. They gently try to introduce or assess the patient's consideration of scenarios that don't go well: death, complications, incomplete recovery, life as an invalid. Does the patient understand the risks? Is there a detailed advance healthcare directive? The question that most struck me was, "Why do you want a transplant?"

That's tantamount to asking a person, "Why do you want to live?" It turns out, it's not such an easy question to answer! Isn't the whole body of religious, philosophical, and mystical thought devoted to this question? There were all kinds of answers I could give: duty and service to others, responsibilities to family, enjoyment of the pleasures of life, unaccomplished goals, contribution to art or academia, etc. I think I stammered out something suitably thoughtful and acceptable, but it's a question that has stayed with me ever since.

There are living donors for some organs, such as kidneys, but for a heart transplant, the donor is deceased. The donor was a person that could very well be me. And after the transplant, in a certain sense, actually _is_ me. It's not really possible to cling to the notion of separateness from other individuals when one's body is not even entirely from a singular genetic heritage. The process of letting go continues. This time, letting go of separateness.

As so often happens, when one has fully embraced and come to love something once avoided, it comes to an end. I so dreaded LVAD implantation. I feared the physical pain of the surgery. But modern painkillers made that manageable. The unexpected hardships were psychological and spiritual. But I accepted it, enjoyed my new progress towards health and vitality, without feeling particular anxiety or urgency about going into transplantation right away. So, naturally, I went almost immediately to transplant.

At the three month mark post-LVAD, I underwent yet another right-heart catheterization, in which I received good news. My pulmonary hypertension had abated—not entirely to normal—but enough to allow my listing as an official cardiac transplant candidate. I was cleared to begin waiting for a donor heart to become available.

Because I'm a medium-sized individual with blood-tissue type AB positive, I'm a universal blood and organ recipient. I can basically accept any healthy organ. I was listed in a high medical priority category as an LVAD recipient, so my doctors assured me that my time waiting for a suitable donor organ would be short. And indeed it was short... only seven days.

Here are the blog entries from the time just prior to my transplant surgery, from my hospital recovery time, and from the weeks and months of home-recovery afterwards. After these blog entries, I will offer some thoughts on the journey from heart failure to transplant, and beyond.

HERMENEUTIC PHENOMENOLOGY
08 MAR 2016

Time marches on. Tuesday, March 22nd will be precisely 12 weeks from my LVAD implantation. It's hard for me to even remember how I felt in the first weeks after that surgery. I do recall that it was painful and difficult, but I can't really access that time. I'm feeling so much stronger and energetic these days, that it is almost as if I never went into advanced heart failure.

March 22nd will also be my fourth right-heart-cath procedure. It will be the moment of truth as to whether the LVAD has been successful in reducing my pulmonary hypertension. If all goes as planned, the cath procedure will show that my pulmonary pressures have dropped to acceptable levels. I can then be listed as a status 1-A or 1-B candidate for cardiac transplantation. Since my blood type is AB positive, and since I'm an individual of average frame size, my actual transplant surgery might be very soon after my listing.

All those thoughts that swirled through my head last fall, when I thought I may be going directly to a transplant surgery (before my detour into LVAD territory), are back once again. Top-of-mind, and in the forefront of my thoughts.

I thought that maybe I was alone in experiencing this existential confusion and dread, but it turns out that there is a lot of literature, and many

scholarly studies about the psychological and philosophical struggles many transplant patients experience... particularly heart transplant patients.

I got lost in the Interweb for a while, drowning in essays, blogs, and research papers. I can't claim to fully understand the flood of concepts I read about. From Husserl and Heidegger, to Sartre and Jean-Luc Nancy, my head has been awhirl with the ideas that form this particular corner of the philosophical landscape. However much or little I do understand of modern philosophy, it is abundantly clear to me that a profound change in my existence is fast approaching.

I had focused for so long on taking one step at a time, that I simply thought of the heart transplant as a simple (albeit painful) event, after which my life would go on as usual.

Actually, it's not that simple. Aside from the lifetime of immune suppression, with its heightened vulnerability to infection, organ rejection, and cancer, there is also an unavoidable adjustment to a new reality.

The fact is, my old life will be over. My heart is simply not capable of sustaining my life any longer. I was able to rely on that organ for 44 years and some months, but no longer. Going forward, only someone else's contribution can make more years of life possible for me. There is no escaping the knowledge that my benefactor, the organ donor, will no longer be alive, except in the sense that one or more of his or her organs may be technically alive in my body and in other organ recipients' bodies.

Our friend Martin has asked if it is possible that the donor could be a woman. And if so, will I become more sensitive and have a better eye for fashion? One can only hope.

So, it will take two people to make each and every minute of post-transplant life possible for me: myself, and my heart donor. But the consequences don't stop there, because there is a third person in the mix: the individual who _didn't_ survive the wait for a donor organ. As long as there are more candidates than donors, then there will be people who run out of time. Others may disagree, but it appears to me that three lives will come to an end, and one post-transplant life will go forward.

I'd rather that my future didn't come at the cost of three lives, and yet I can make no apologies. Like most people, my greed for life is fierce and primal. I love being alive, and there's not much I wouldn't do to grasp at every moment I can. I can only be grateful that, in life, the provider of my eventual new heart elected to become an organ donor.

Why does this matter at all? I have come to this conclusion: there is a little bit of extra weight to the question I've often asked myself in the past, and that I will continue to ask from time to time in the future (as we all do in one way or another). Instead of merely asking Plato's question, "Am I living a good life?", my question becomes "Am I living a life good enough for three?"

PULMONARY PRESSURES DOWN ...
READY FOR TRANSPLANT LISTING
24 MAR 2016

The right heart catheterization yesterday (March 23rd) went ahead very smoothly. They went through the brachial vein (crook of the right elbow) this time, instead of the jugular. So it was really painless and easy. The prep time and waiting for the cath lab took a lot longer than the actual procedure.

There has been a dramatic improvement in the last three months, as the LVAD has done its job heroically. My pulmonary hypertension is entirely within acceptable levels, so now I'm ready for listing as a status 1-B cardiac transplant candidate. Category 1-B is the second-highest medical priority. So from April 1st, I will be in a waiting state. Waiting for that call from UCSF that a donor heart is available, get your ass into the hospital NOW!

How long will that be? Honestly, no one knows. Probably a few months, although it could potentially be a lot less. The good news is that I've recovered from the LVAD implantation very well, and now feel great. So while I would like to get on with the next operation, I'm not on any particular timeline governed by medical necessity.

We'll continue with life as usual, making plans with friends and family (local to the SF area, of course), but with the caveat that those plans could be cancelled at any time, if I need to rush to the hospital. In the meantime, bring on the vino (in moderation, naturally)!

GULP... GOING IN FOR TRANSPLANT TONIGHT
31 MAR 2016

I knew I was bumped up to Status 1A listing yesterday (after a week listed as status 1-B), but I did NOT expect a donor heart to become available the next day. I just got the call at 10:00 am. I'm to check in at 4:00 pm for prep. I believe the operation will begin at around 7pm. It's a 6-12 hour procedure, depending on any possible, as-yet-unknown issues in either the donor organ or in my chest cavity.

There is a chance that upon visual inspection of the donor heart at 5:00 pm this evening, that an unexpected problem presents itself to make the donor organ unusable. So there is a possibility that the whole thing is called off last minute. But I'm obviously hoping the organ is pristine and that we can move ahead full speed.

I don't know any details about the donor, except that it is a 29-year-old, with a clean health history. I will probably be able to find out the sex of the donor, but nothing else. Privacy is very carefully maintained.

My hands are cold and shaking as I write this post, and I can hardly think at all. There are a million things to do before going in this afternoon. Stephanie will post updates as they become available. Wish my surgical team good luck!

OUT OF THE OR AND INTO ICU
01 APR 2016 (ENTRY BY STEPHANIE)

Manu's heart transplant surgery went well last night. He was transferred into the cardiac ICU at around 4am. As of the writing of this post, he's still sedated and intubated. They plan on waking him up slowly this morning, taking out the breathing tube and then seeing how he responds. If he's responsive and not in too much pain, they may have him sit in a chair and/or take a short walk in the ICU. Crazy to think about a stroll (!) within 24 hours of a heart transplant, but movement and being upright helps the body get back to normal faster.

He should be in the ICU for around three days. Then, he'll be transferred to a room on the cardiac floor, where due to his LVAD surgery three short months ago, he already knows all the nurses, and they know him. In fact, when being prepped for surgery on the floor, we received lots of hugs and well wishes from the nurses we knew. The very supportive mechanical/LVAD team was also there and stayed with him in the OR until the very last second when his heart and LVAD were taken out of his chest. We anticipate he'll stay two weeks in the hospital after leaving ICU.

Amit, Manu's brother, is flying in from Miami today and will help out with managing his care for the next few days. We hope to avoid some of the physical and mental complications that Manu experienced during his LVAD recovery. That said, we don't anticipate any major issues. He's in very, very good care.

Thanks to everyone for reaching out and sending your wishes, prayers, smiley faces and heart emoticons, devas and all around good vibes to Manu and me.

And one last note: for his post-recovery viewing pleasure, Manu asked that photos be taken of his heart (now, his "former" heart) and the donor heart (now, his "new" heart). If they were indeed taken, he may share those with whomever wants to see them. More later.

*** *Manu's note a year after transplant* ***

Sonia did indeed take some photographs in the ER of both my old heart after being taken out of my chest, as well as the new donor heart before it was implanted. I didn't include these photos in the blog, in case anyone was squeamish, but I am including them here.

The old heart is on the left. Note the LVAD pump assembly sticking out the bottom of the heart (top of the photograph). Notice how large, distended, and terrible-looking the organ is. There was just no muscle tone left, and was not capable of sustaining life any longer. The beautiful donor heart is on the right. It is small, the size of a fist, and solid, smooth muscle. It is a pale white-ish color in the photo because all of the blood has been flushed out, and it is immersed in a preserving fluid. The old heart must implanted in a new body within 20-40 hours to be viable.

POST TRANSPLANT DAYS 1 & 2 IN ICU
02 APR 2016 (ENTRY BY STEPHANIE)

This is a quick update on what went on in ICU yesterday, Friday, and anticipations for today. I won't be writing a post every day, but I know that everyone is anxious to know how his first few days are going with a new heart.

Yesterday, around 11am – 7 hours after leaving the OR – they extubated him (took out the breathing tube that went down his trachea). This allowed him to speak a bit and to breathe on his own. Also, they reduced his sedation. About an hour or so later, he was fairly alert and speaking more. He still had oxygen and nitrite given to him via a nasal cannula (the plastic tube thingy that goes into your nostrils).

The transplant surgeon came by for a visit and told us that the surgery went really well without any complications, and that the donor heart was "jumping" and very healthy. He explained the protocol for the drug regimen while in the hospital. This is what UCSF has pioneered over the years and has helped to give them a nearly 100% success rate with heart transplants.

In the afternoon, Manu sat in a chair for several hours, which is vital to wake up his lungs, other organs and bowels after such a major surgery. His pain was managed with IV Tylenol and he had a few bouts of nausea. Nothing unusual to report. His brother Amit was a great help with getting information from the staff and recommending alternative drugs to help with pain and nausea, since these were more than likely the culprit for his delirium during his LVAD recovery.

The surgeon established a heart rate of 110 (ordinarily around 85) via an epicardial pacemaker, which is an external machine that is hooked up to wires that go directly into his heart in two places. Called "pacing", this keeps the right heart pressures down, reducing the chance of the new heart failing. It will remain in place for 4-5 days.

Also, another piece of info: his heart has had regular heartbeats immediately and this supposedly is only the case of 25% of the new heart transplants at UCSF. So far, this has been a very good, strong heart.

In the evening, he was up for several hours talking, joking with the staff, and threatening to go raving in the ICU tomorrow. Lastly, they started him on anti-rejection drugs and steroids. These will be gradually reduced to minimal levels, but never eliminated. Manu will be on a cocktail of drugs for the rest of his life. And yes, he will be on the pregnant woman's diet the rest of his life: no oysters, sushi, or unpasteurized foods. Thankfully, drinking will be allowed later on. Whew!

Today, Saturday, he is even more lucid. He took a walk and was steady – not raving yet, but still impressive less than 36 hours after a heart transplant. His pain has increased so they will control that as needed. He may have a small meal, starting with the BRAT diet; my Peace Corps friends know this diet intimately! Other projects for today will include weaning him off the oxygen and nitrate, doing lung exercises to expand his lung capacity, and taking out one of his many IV lines.

If no issues arise with rejection (and none are anticipated), this heart should keep Manu alive for decades. We are so grateful to the donor, his/her family and the UCSF team for this extraordinary gift.

Okay, many people are texting, calling, sending telepathic messages asking how they can help. Here are two options:

1) **Donate blood.** It's simple, easy, and relaxing. Afterwards, you get free juice!
   http://www.redcrossblood.org/donating-blood
   http://www.bloodcenters.org/

2) **Become an organ donor,** if you're not already. One donor can save as many as eight lives. Manu is very, very fortunate to be one of the lives saved by a donor organ. If you want to become a donor, make sure that decision is noted on your driver's license and on your living will/medical directive, and that your family is aware of your wishes.
   http://www.organdonor.gov/becomingdonor/stateregistries.html

And again, our undying gratitude to everyone for your steadfast love and support!

MANU OUT OF ICU
05 APR 2016 (ENTRY BY STEPHANIE)

Time in the ICU sped by without any major issues. Manu was transferred to the regular cardiac floor on Monday evening and he was even able to walk the 400 feet to his new room, which has a million dollar view of San Francisco and the Bay. Many thanks to the wonderful cardiac ICU nurses who made his stay there as comfortable as possible.

Manu's team of doctors are very happy with his progress and are optimistic that he'll be going home sooner rather than later. We may have an idea of his discharge date at the end of this week. However, you never know what can happen (he had a heart transplant, after all!), so we're just taking it day by day.

FOR EVERY ATOM BELONGING TO ME
AS GOOD BELONGS TO YOU...
09 APR 2016
— Walt Whitman, *Song of Myself*

Day Nine. I could not possibly ask for more… from life, from the universe. There is another human being's heart thumping in my chest right now as I type these words. Today, I had the last intravenous line disconnected from me, and was able to shower. Paradise!

I have been walking several times a day for the past week. Very little pain to speak of. No bouts of insanity. My recovery has been textbook-smooth. To the point that my doctors talk more about Anderson Cooper's book tour than about my medical condition. Believe me, it's good for your doctors to be bored with your case.

I am now in the process of getting my anti-rejection drugs saturated into my body at the right concentrations, while keeping the other systems like the kidneys and liver from rebelling. We could use John Kerry up in here. Should be home in four days, which would make my total stay 14 days... just as they predicted. I must say, the transplant team at UCSF must get tired of being right all the time. I know just how they feel, since I'm right all the time myself.

It's hard to describe exactly how I feel, but it has been a profound experience every step of the way. The pain and fear, hope and relief, euphoria and sadness all wash together. All I can really say is that I feel profoundly Alive. And the sheer audacity of that fact stops me, right in my tracks, several times a day. I have been technically dead twice (once at LVAD implantation, and again at transplant), and my third life is off to a great start.

All I can do these days is let poetry work its magic. It's the only thing that has been able to give me a way to access my own experience of existence. Walt Whitman's *"Song of Myself"* from **Leaves of Grass** has been the recurring, serendipitous touchstone of my journey, lately. The poems just kept coming up over and over, in all different contexts, for the last few weeks.

In fact, the last thing I requested from Sonia (who is on the LVAD/MCS team) as I went under anesthetic was to hear Walt's magnificent words lead me out of one life and into another. Charlene, my anesthesiologist, was able to find a recitation online, and played it for me on her iPhone. It was a great comfort. I fought my sedation for a couple minutes until I heard the line, "I sound my barbaric yawp over the rooftops of the world...", and then I let myself sink into sleep. I awoke with a new life and a new heart banging thunderously in my chest.

Mostly, I think about the donor whose heart is now part of me, and whose other organs are providing life for perhaps as many as seven other

fortunate people. I keep returning to the last lines of *Song of Myself*. It's
what I would offer to the donor's family as they mourn:

STANZA 52

I depart as air, I shake my white locks at the runaway sun,
I effuse my flesh in eddies, and drift it in lacy jags.

I bequeath myself to the dirt to grow from the grass I love,
If you want me again look for me under your boot-soles.

You will hardly know who I am or what I mean,
But I shall be good health to you nevertheless,
And filter and fibre your blood.

Failing to fetch me at first keep encouraged,
Missing me one place search another,
I stop somewhere waiting for you.

HOME AGAIN! TEN DAYS IN THE HOSPITAL
11 APR 2016

Just a quick update folks, to let you know that I got sprung out of jail a
bit early for good behavior. My recovery has been going so well that all of
my IV's, pacing lines, chest-tubes, etc. were removed by Friday April
8th. So, on Sunday, my docs asked the same question I've been asking
(much to Stephanie's disapproval)… why am I still here in the hospital?

So happily, I'm home! A ten-day recovery stay in the hospital post-
transplant is pretty good. It will not surprise anyone to hear that I love being
back home. Still fairly weak, but getting stronger. Taking naps, eating well,
etc. Adjusting to my 51 pills a day. I expect to start working again in a few
days as well.

For the next 6-8 weeks, I will be going to UCSF every morning, except Tuesdays, for blood draws, biopsies, and clinic appointments. That will taper off to eventually only being a couple times a year and monthly blood draws. But for a while, I'll be a frequent sight at the UCSF Transplant Center.

Continued thanks to everyone, from both Stephanie and me, for all the visits and food and good wishes! See you on the dance floor!

ONE MONTH POST TRANSPLANT... IT'S A RUFF LIFE
28 APR 2016

It's been exactly 28 days since the transplant. Lots of folks have asked for an update, so I suppose I should haul my carcass off the bed and over to the computer. It's been terrific at home, and Stephanie chauffeurs me all over the place (mostly back to UCSF for blood draws, biopsies, and clinic visits).

The recovery is going well, if a bit slowly. I'm told that my suppressed immune system makes the healing process slower than it might ordinarily be. I've had a few challenges, including a brief two-day readmission to the hospital a couple weeks ago, for fears of an infection. None of the many tests came back positive, so we'll never know what exactly it was. I returned home after two days, and continued my gradual strengthening regimen, which consists of eating and sleeping.

Stella and Enzo have been keeping me company, and many people have come to visit, sent cards, or called. Thank you everyone, for your kind wishes! Nothing dramatic to report.

During this coming month (Month 2 after transplant), my biopsies drop to bi-weekly instead of weekly. I'll be able to drive again in a couple weeks, and maybe I'll have a reduction in blood-draw-frequency (currently 3 times a week).

By the way, the results of my 4 biopsies so far have been: 1-R, 0-R, 1-R, 0-R. All good. No overt signs of rejection. 0-R means no signs of rejection whatsoever. A biopsy result of 1-R means signs of inflammation, but no rejection. If a result ever came back as 2R, then active steps to increase immuno-suppressive therapy would be called for. So far, so good.

I've started to get back to work a couple hours a day (between UCSF visits and naps). Hoping to add more and more "normal" life activities in the coming weeks. Have to go take 18 pills now....

TWO MILLION DOLLAR MAN
16 JUN 2016

It's been 77 days since transplant. About six months from my first hospitalization last November. Two surgeries. An LVAD. A new heart. 10 right-heart catheterizations, including 7 biopsies. 36 nights in a hospital. Something like 75 blood draws. And _at least_ $2.6 million in billed costs (so far).

Things continue to go very well indeed. I'm back to work full time. I can walk 3 miles or more at a time, and have started cardiac rehab. That's a monitored workout, twice a week. My medical chores have dropped down in frequency quite a bit. I'm now down to once-a-month biopsies and clinic visits, and that will likely decrease even more in the next month. Blood draws are now every two weeks, going to monthly.

So now as my attention on recovery lessens in favor of the ordinary business of life, I'm happy to report that there has been no rejection so far, and I'm very optimistic that I'll continue to feel better and better going forward. I'm told by the transplant team at UCSF that everything is looking good, and that I should continue to feel better with each passing month. This gradual improvement will continue right through the one year mark, until my health will hardly impact my lifestyle, except for continuing medications and being vigilant against infection due to immune suppression.

I expect that there will now be very infrequent blog posts. I may still throw some random thoughts and philosophical musings up here, but I won't send newsletters to clog your inboxes every time I do.

And once again, thank you to everyone for your fond wishes, for your support, and for your many kindnesses during this difficult six months. Thanks especially to the terrific team at the UCSF Transplant Center. It's not possible to overstate the grandeur of the work that they do there every day.

As I write this section, it is now nearly nine months since my transplant. Recovery for every patient varies greatly, and I feel grateful that I've had minimal setbacks. I've talked to patients that have experienced post-transplant kidney failure, those that have had rejection episodes, infections, prolonged hospital stays, and more. But many patients have also had smooth recoveries like I did.

I've only had one re-hospitalization since my discharge. That was for a bought of weakness and fever one week after my initial discharge. As a precaution, my doctors insisted I return for a couple days while they pumped every known course of antibiotics through my IV, and ran every bacterial and viral infection test they could. Never did find out what it was, but I felt better after 2 days, so they sent me home.

After about six weeks, the booming of my new heart also seemed to quiet down. From the moment I woke up from anesthesia, I heard a roaring in my ears. My new heart seemed to boom. It was a new, joyous sound that often kept me awake for a while, before I could fall asleep each night. It might simply be a result of the pericardial sac being cut open for the transplant surgery. I was told that inflammation makes it impossible to sew back together when closing up after the transplant, so it's just left to gradually close on its own (with scar tissue) in the weeks after transplant. Perhaps that's why my heart seemed pound so thunderously, at first.

Aside from the volume, a transplanted heart also runs very fast. A resting heart rate for a healthy adult might be around 70 beats per minute. My resting heart rate is 95-97 bpm. The donor heart is completely *denervated* (no nerve connections), including the vagus nerve, which is responsible for slowing the heartrate when not in fight-or-flight mode. I'm told that this is quite normal, and doesn't have any real impact on daily life for the transplant recipient, except for requiring some care to warm up into exercise.

It hasn't been all sunshine and songbirds, but progress has been very steady. I was surprised that once I got home, I didn't radically and exponentially improve, as I had after my LVAD surgery. One of my doctors suggested that high immune suppression would slow down all of my recovery and healing times. That certainly seems the case for me. I had trouble gauging my own energy reserves. If I skipped my afternoon nap, I paid for it by needing to spend the next day in bed, shivering and weak. But those bouts of weakness diminished, and after six weeks, I hardly even needed those naps anymore. I still like them, though, so I sneak them in whenever I can.

Fortunately for transplant patients, things get easier very quickly. Initially, there is an extreme regimen that takes you back to the hospital 4 out 5 days of the week: blood draws (3 per week), heart tissue biopsies via catheterization (1 per week), and clinic visits (1 per month). Over time, the blood draws drop to one per week, then every other week, then monthly. Biopsies drop from weekly, to bi-weekly, to monthly, to quarterly, to never. There is a wonderful test called Allomap (created by the life-sciences company, CareDx), that employs a simple blood sample to test for early genetic indicators of rejection. Once the transplant center has determined that the biopsy results have been well-correlated by the Allomap results, biopsies are eventually discontinued. A huge relief!

Medication also drops off over time. Dosages of certain of the multiple immune suppression reduces. Prednisone is stepped down over six months, and then discontinued (testing for rejection with biopsies at every reduction in dosage). Once Prednisone is eliminated, about four other prophylactic treatments can also be discontinued. I'm down from 52 pills per day to 32. It will probably stay around that level for life, but it's easier than I thought it would be to keep on top of the logistics. Like everything else, you adjust and get good at what needs doing.

One of the most strongly recommended elements of post-transplant recovery (at least by UCSF) is cardiac rehabilitation for rebuilding strength and stamina. That's a 36 session course of monitored work-outs, overseen by a team of nurses and exercise physiologists. I started out with very mild treadmill walking and stationary bike. The staff at CPMC (California Pacific Medical Center) where I went, was terrific, and monitored all their cardiac patients very carefully—with telemetry for the first 6 weeks to monitor sinus rhythm, and always with frequent blood pressure and heart rate measurements.

Like every patient after an open heart procedure, I felt very tentative about exercise. I felt shaky and weak, didn't know what my limits were, and definitely was very protective of my chest. I walked around everywhere with hunched shoulders. At cardiac rehab, we learned from the staff how to get our confidence, balance, and strength back. They also tailored a workout program for me that had me jogging for short periods within 4 weeks, beginning light weight training, and then increasing the duration of the runs.

I'm happy to say that I gained confidence quickly, and now maintain my workouts on my own. I still lift weights, and can now easily jog 3-4 miles at a clip, although quite slowly (12:40 mile pace is my best 5K so far). My goal of running 3-5 miles at a 10-minute mile pace now looks achievable. Maybe I'll make it to the Transplant Games in 2018!

In addition to the physical recovery, there's a big psychological adjustment that all of us transplant recipients need to go through. Everything is different. I feel as if my old self is gone. I'm not sure what this new self is, but things are not the same. One of the funny common factoids about transplant patients in general, and heart transplant patients in particular, is that many of us no longer feel a special affinity for our birthdays. I used always feel like May 22nd was my day, but this year, it didn't hold that resonance for me. It can be difficult, because everyone around me still views me as Manu, but that person may not exist anymore.

In many cultures around the world, big life transitions are marked by a ceremony, and the ritual taking of a new name. It's not a bad way to acknowledge the reality of a significant life change. I'm not sure if I'm quite ready to go down to the courthouse and make Siddhartha Raindance Goldstein Velasquez a reality, so I'll just keep things as they are... for now.

Those of us who have been lucky enough to be given a second chance at life by an organ transplantation think a lot about our donors. And their families. It's such a traumatic ordeal for the donor's family to have lost their loved one, and to have to give consent for the donation of their loved one's organs. Their privacy is quite rightly protected, but there is a mechanism through which we organ recipients can send letters of condolence to the donor families.

A wonderful volunteer from Donor Network West gave a talk to my VAD/transplant support group, and she mentioned that while only about half of the donor families respond to a letter of condolence, all of them greatly appreciate receiving such a letter. It's often the one small comfort they can take, knowing that at least some good came from their great loss. There's no timetable for when to write and send such a letter. For me, I thought about it constantly, but couldn't put pen to paper for six months. Even after writing it, I let it sit for a couple more months, scared I was not saying the right things.

But I did want them to know how grateful I was for their sacrifice, and how seriously I took the responsibility for caring for their loved one's heart as my own. So, I sent my condolence letter, via the network of social workers. Who knows? Perhaps they will respond and tell me more about this person whose heart has given me life. Of course I want to know everything about her or him. For me, writing the letter was an important milestone in my healing and recovery process.

While I feel wonderfully alive these days, I don't feel as if I've vanquished an enemy, or feel victorious in any way. I don't really feel any truth in the "fighting" and "battle" metaphors for what I've gone through with my personal death and rebirth. Can I really blame my own heart for failing me? After all, it gave everything it had to give, for 44 years.

No, I didn't "overcome" anything. Many people helped me, and I was forced to let go of a lot of illusions. I surrendered to the reality that I was profoundly weak, sick, and dying. I relied on other people's support and expertise. I did the reasonable and prudent things for my recovery, like taking meds and listening to doctors' orders. And of course, I was just plain lucky in a lot of ways.

There's nothing but tenderness and great affection in me, for my poor old heart. The bruised and battered pump that served me so valiantly for so many years. Maybe the language of war is helpful to other people, to other patients. But it was never a metaphor that worked for me, and I wonder how truly it works for others.

When I told him about my heart transplant experience, my good friend and mentor Carl exclaimed that I had been through Joseph Campbell's archetypal hero's journey. This is the description Joseph Campbell made of the universal myth of the hero that seems to cut across all cultures and languages. It's the journey from ignorance and helplessness, to experience and complete agency. Along the way, the hero encounters a number of specific challenges, events, and tests... including a metaphysical death-and-rebirth by going through a dark cave or body of water (think of Jonah in the belly of the whale, or Luke Skywalker in the trash compactor). In the end, the hero's journey is only complete after a literal or symbolic confrontation with one's father (or father-figure).

Well, it's true that I've been technically dead and revived a couple of times. And it's also true, in a way, that I've been forced to confront my father—or at least his genetic illness. I can see why my friend thought of this archetype when hearing about my heart transplant journey. I think he was quite astute in seeing this parallel. What's especially striking to me, is that, according to Campbell, the _end_ of the hero's journey is merely the _start_ of his adult life.

So, what now? Quo vadis? Where to go from here? I haven't the foggiest notion, and that's just how I like it. It's quite delicious to not know the future, to not know any limits.

Now that I sit at my first anniversary of transplantation, it's crystal clear that I've been the recipient of the gift of a second life. The journey has been one of transformation, death, and rebirth. In a way, it has been a physical, visceral, and involuntary echo of the Buddhist path of awakening into self-knowledge.

I leave you now with a couple of thoughts that have become touchstones for me in my new life.

First, the principle of non-separation, of non-identity. As a transplant recipient, it's impossible for me to ignore the reality that there is no such thing as Me. That it's difficult to set a boundary between "Me" and "Not-Me". After all, there is someone else's heart in the center of my body, keeping me/us alive every second. I believe that this principle of non-separateness actually holds true for everyone, and is only a bit more black-and-white for a transplant recipient.

In fact, by numbers of cells, all of us are at least 50% other organisms, like the bacteria on or inside our bodies. It has become clear to researchers recently that this human microbiota is absolutely essential for life and health. So where do we really draw the line between ourselves, and everyone else? everything else? Maybe that line doesn't really exist.

Second, the allegory of the Heracletian fire. This is the famous set of analogies by the Greek historian-philosopher Heracletus, who stated that permanence was an illusion, that all things are in flux. He likened the universe to a great, cosmic fire, which is constantly burning, but never the same from instant to instant. Famously, he stated that one can never step into the same river twice. By the time one steps into a river and removes one's foot, the water will have flowed on downstream, to be replaced by new water from upstream. What we might view as the "same" river is, in fact, composed of entirely new water from instant to instant, just like all of the cosmos.

Our cells do the very same thing all the time. They constantly die and are replaced by new cells. Every seven years or so, there is not a single cell in our bodies that was the same as seven years prior. To me, this transience, impermanence, and constant renewal of our bodies reflects the state of all reality. It's what physicists have been saying for at least the last century— the equivalence of matter and energy, the wave-particle duality of all matter, etc. The universe seems more an _unfolding occurrence_, not a _thing that exists_.

Non-identity, unity with all things, transience, and relentless,-constant change. These are the terrible and sublime lessons of the journey from heart failure to transplantation.

It has been just over a year past transplant, and I'm happy to say that life with a transplanted heart can be amazingly rich. Six weeks after my transplant surgery, I struggled to merely walk for 20 minutes without a rest-stop. I still had incision pain, and tenderness at the healing breast-bone. Jogging a decent distance seemed a distance goal, at best.

But with encouragement and support at cardiac rehab twice a week for 18 weeks, I was able to add two minutes of slow jogging to my walking treadmill regimen. Then three minutes, then five. We added light weight training. Progress was very slow, and sometimes a cold or general fatigue cost a whole week of no working out. But still, improvement was steady.

And now? I'm able to run 4-5 times per week, gradually increasing distances to the 3-4 mile level now. I'm hoping to continue this upward progress, and it feels like an incredible gift. After years of being unable to run at all during heart failure, I can't believe this is even possible, never mind fun. My friend Ron and I just ran in a charity event, the Levi's Guardsmen Presidio10. We did the five-kilometer distance (3.1 miles) in 36'38" (a steady 11'47"  mile pace)! A week later at another 5K event, the American Heart Association Brazen Western Pacific, I managed to even beat this time with a nice 36'16" finish. Next year's goal is to regularly run 10km distances at less than 65 minute times. Seems like a stretch, but we'll see!

Finally, I close this account with our dear friend Heidi's favorite poem, which always makes me think of my organ donor, and her/his family:

[i carry your heart with me(i carry it in]
BY E. E. CUMMINGS

i carry your heart with me(i carry it in
my heart)i am never without it(anywhere
i go you go,my dear;and whatever is done
by only me is your doing,my darling)
                    i fear
no fate(for you are my fate,my sweet)i want
no world(for beautiful you are my world,my true)
and it's you are whatever a moon has always meant
and whatever a sun will always sing is you

here is the deepest secret nobody knows
(here is the root of the root and the bud of the bud
and the sky of the sky of a tree called life;which grows
higher than soul can hope or mind can hide)
and this is the wonder that's keeping the stars apart

i carry your heart(i carry it in my heart)

Made in the USA
Coppell, TX
21 September 2020 ·

38522817R00042